COMPOSTING AT FORTY

COMPOSTING AT FORTY
AND
OTHER POEMS

by

Ron McFarland

Confluence Press, Inc.
at
Lewis-Clark State College
Lewiston, Idaho

ACKNOWLEDGMENTS

Several poems in this volume have been drawn from three earlier compilations: *Certain Women* (Confluence Press, 1977), *Not to Worry* (Audit Poetry, 1978), and *Eight Idaho Poets* (University Press of Idaho, 1979).

Poems have also been reprinted from the following magazines: *Hampden-Sydney Poetry Review, Poetry Northwest, Mississippi Mud, Amphora Review, Blue Unicorn, Slackwater Review, New Jersey Poetry Journal, Confrontation, Berkeley Poetry Review, Coe Review, Aag,Aag!, Spoon River Quarterly, Kavitha, New Laurel Review, Connecticut Quarterly, New Letters, Yarrow, Indiana Review, Wind, Poetry Now, Quarterly West, Descant, Southern Poetry Review, Poem, Tightrope, Bellingham Review, Limberlost Review, West Coast Poetry Review, River Bottom, Willow Springs, Webster Review, Clearwater Journal, Impact.*

A few of the poems have been revised (I hope for the better) since their original appearance in print.

Cover and illustrations from George Wither, *A Collection of Emblemes*, 1635. English Emblem Books #12, Series edited by John Horden for Scolar Press, 1968, Menston, Yorkshire, England.

Emblems themselves actually done by members of the van De Baffle family of engravers from the Netherlands.

For My Parents

CONTENTS

1.

2.

3.

4.

5.

He that delights to Plant *and* Set,
Makes After-Ages *in his* Debt.

POET IN RESIDENCE

Who is your modern poetry man
is rather what is your modern poetry man
is the fellow with the dark mad hair
and fluffy mustache
leaning over there against the wall
looking tweedy and seedy all at once
and wondering about his book and tenure
and the look of a browneyed coed
and where the next poem is coming from.

SOME OF YOU

This semester we have an enormous text,
but of course we will not read all of it.
Some of you will prove you know it all
in only a few weeks, at least to your own
satisfaction, so you will stop
let's say at Chapter Two, before anything
really good even begins to happen. But
that's how it will be for some of you.
Some of you are like that, always
knowing in advance what to avoid,
or avoiding what others must endure,
yet somehow getting by. Your friends
are of short duration, like quick
shots of whiskey, but nothing for you
goes down smoothly. Some of you will
not come back from this mission.
Some of you should not even be here,
you're just green kids from Kansas.
Some of you don't even know what love
and beauty are. For some of you
there is no excuse unless you can
find it somewhere in this enormous text.

AN INFORMAL DISCUSSION WITH
THE PHI BETA KAPPA LECTURER

When the visiting scholar raised his arms
and linked his fingers, forming two wings
behind his learned head,
we saw his airline tickets
flashing blue and red.

Already then, two highballs to the wind,
he soars above us
cruising altitudes beyond our sight,
his smile accusing us of our decision
not to come aboard,
and of our grounded imprecision.

One of us tries a question
and he loops the loop, performs a barrel-roll.
We gasp, we nod
and someone scrapes a chair,
and someone yawns,
and then we all applaud.

MATTHEW HOPKINS (d. 1647): MAN OF PRINCIPLE

It was wrong, what they said of us,
how we stripped and threatened,
thumbscrewed, pricked a vengeance
into their soft white virgin
skin until confession
dribbled from their ruby lips.

Can't you see where blood
crusts neither tip of these pincers?
where gore splatters
not a single board of the rack?
how my own eye-gouger
stiffens from disuse?

Wives and mothers, we adored them
to a fault, in Mary's name,
for blest Veronica, Susanna
with the elders in her silken gown
billowing over trim ankles
like a sail on Galilee, tricky
Rebecca, Jezebel, Jael
of nail and hammer
enjoyed by Sisera just before
he died, Delilah, gloating Deborah,
Noah's wife, Salome's mother.

These women. They will suck your soul
right through their bat's wing lips.
They will grip your testicles
with a wolf's tenacity until
your semen drips
a sterile yellow,

mandrakes howling from the ground
under a shrunken lemon moon.
These women, cackling love
to goats and rats, swoon
on the stench of their own cauldrons.

Who do you think those goats and rats
once were? Why does the mole
look manly in the face? What simian
fool will you become,
clutching some wench's ragged hem?
I swear we never touched them.

GARDENING

In your garden as in life it is always the same,
the wind rattles the sweet golden corn
still green in their stalks, young
vascular bundles rich in their tissues
flexed erect into time, their heads
heavy with sex.
                         Beneath his ribs
Sir Thomas wished it could be so with him,
the harmony of the wind's four corners, breath
of the Holy Ghost, a soft Platonic gust
from anther to stigma. Just
release of pollen,
                         then he might step back
and let the pistils do their work, observe
such harmonies as time and chance permit,
then harvest like a savage.
                         And is this then
the foolishest act, this trivial insertion,
vulgar sowing, bursting open
liberation of the seed, scattered so often
in the dark, the clock ticking, ticking
like a clown's calculated grin, the ridicule,
your paradoxical pants down?
                         Sometimes it's hard
to be a scholar and a scientist, lopped
from people who embrace each other
with no more thought than pollen

clinging to a fly's wing, happy never knowing,
after all, exactly how or why the yellow petals
of tulips pressed against your garden suddenly
grow pallid, shrivel, fall.

WELDING

Boilermaker, ironworker, plumber, millwright,
steamfitter, work in heat and grit
fusing piece to piece
                 the broken things
of the world.
            Behind your mask the sweat
beads, trickles. Behind your goggled eyes
dreams of bridges bloom,
helium flowers,
           Pipeline nightmares.
Somewhere north of Fairbanks
her letter reaches you,
               dull pink roses
on a cold afternoon, pieces
you cannot fuse.

"FILL 'ER UP, MAC"

At Mr. Finch's in 1946 we bought
a dozen eggs and a tank so full of gas
it lasted all the way to Florida
and 1968.
Mr. Finch believed his eggs were better,
warm from hens he knew by their first names,
believed in the mysterious virtues
of Pennsylvania oil (where it was discovered,
he told us once, by William Penn),
believed his golden scallop
stood for better gasoline,
unwatered, fresh, high octane rated, clean.

Stoney always hired a slow, blue-eyed
high school graduate and a fast imbecile,
something for everyone.
On busy days the loafers would drop their pop bottles,
catch a few windshields
for customers of the preferred sex.
His expert mechanic, on from eight till six,
could almost fix your car, he was that good.
He knew the mysteries beneath the hood,
or if he didn't now, he'd wink,
by tomorrow he would.

Let us lament the passing of these simple men,
replaced by pumps that need no winding,
by gasoline of unknown origins

promiscuously commingling underground,
by stations where no outstretched line will ping
to warn the loafers at the Coke machine
we have arrived.
Another twenty years, or ten, it will not matter
that your lipstick's smeared or that
since you last wore those shorts you've gotten fatter.

HAVE FUN?

We are getting drunk. The music
is like the war, your bombs
vaguely scattering among docile cows.
You keep asking for "Tuxedo Junction"
and each time it plays you laugh,
maybe remembering that blockbuster
that blew up the swastika factory.
That was Dorsey, that was Miller, this is whiskey.

We aren't having fun. These women,
they are all grey and they keep on
getting greyer whenever you touch them.
The waitresses, especially the young blondes,
turn greyest of all, and quickest.
Good friends' wives are always grey,
and greyest just before they fade away.

Tomorrow we'll fish the Clearwater,
and the water will be grey. We'll drink
coffee, rub our heads, swear off
these funny drunks. We'll talk
about anything but women, Italy,
Glenn Miller, food, and poetry.
You will drive to Montana alone,
tell everyone there that you had fun.

AT SIXTY

Life becomes a curiosity,
the way squirrels dart for popcorn
or the way your popcorn breaks
between arthritic fingers. Or just
this morning how your finger
found itself triggering a coffee cup
at an oriental waiter.

And then each hour matters,
the frustration of water fountains,
the lack of cooperation
organ to organ, one hand to the other,
sarcasm of boys, and worse,
indifference of young women
folding their arms across their sex
as if your stare
could wither their suppleness.

Yet with all this your senses rise
like young animals, your thinning skin
caresses everything it touches,
the edges of love carved
in park benches, or the silken blossoms
of gardenias browning in your hand.

Slim fingers slip away from your clasp.
The war confuses itself with films
about the war or books about the war.
Three memories from Morotai reserved
for such occasions: the heat, mosquitoes,
no Japs. It must be hard,
someone says, living these days
on a fixed income.

OLD POET NEAR FAIRBANKS

Nothing's funny in the snow.
It is too cold to more than smile
dimly as a char's
shadow under the ice.
Silences loom between syllables,
mute seagulls, snow white
winter gray and black.
Glaciers lodge at the back of the throat,
vowels prevail in the polar wind
whispering cold, narrow
thoughts at his threshold.

In spring, iambic as a swung axe,
his lines run quiet. Blood
seeps from the flanks of a bull elk,
wolves test his age
in a tightening circle.
Anapestic woodpeckers
work gray spruce stumps for worms.
In a pine-panelled tavern
the old poet hunches over his bourbon
waiting for something warm to happen.

UNCLE CRAIG'S SHARKSKIN SHOES

Sharks wear shoes in their stomachs,
just one or two
                from young sailors
sunk in the deep blue sea,
                from old skippers
down with their clipper ships,
             from pirates,
             French and Spanish,
     briny boots thick with polish
swallowed to the clink
of salty gold doubloons.
        Digesting black beards
        flesh and tarsals,
        all but beltbuckles and barnacles,
sharks feed on almost anything,
but they prefer romance and raw meat.

Behold, you may, the Picture, here;
Of what, keepes Man, and Childe, in feare.

CERTAIN WOMEN

Women like that cannot stand tenderness.
Not of their flesh,
                    your soft caress
wears like a cold stare.
Velvet over larynx, skin over granite
their voices quarry hard words,
                    worry in garnet,
                    grief in jade,
no remorse. Your sympathy
grates on the air.
Women like that prefer brief farewells.
Not to their taste,
                    your lingering
where dew licks the leaf.

OTHER WOMEN

Rarely beautiful they
cling to the outer rim
of your best fantasies.
They wear satin, watered
silk and they dance slowly,
footloose in memory.
By day they are nothing.
Sun dissolves them like
a child's tongue on lemon,
strawberry, melon, lime,
the family of ices.
These priceless women are
just barely tangible,
quick touches, kisses that
don't quite happen, sometimes
words, barely beautiful.

THE LENTIL QUEEN

Heir apparent to the peas,
you ease the hard red wheat
beneath your combine
green as a crown jewel,
jasmine cigarettes censing the cab.

What does your wheat whisper
under a cold half moon?
"Remember Ceres beautiful as you.
We feel her presence in our roots,
feel her pain in your sickle. Beware."

Smiling through this myth
you choose to reap the lentils,
glean a circle in the yellow rape.
Farmers across the ridge
scratch their heads, what does it mean?

You bend the brim of your leather hat.
"I have my beauty. I fear nothing.
Tomorrow I disc the wheat stubble
quietly, relentless. What does it mean?
I flourish. I am the lentil queen."

PORTRAIT OF AN INDEPENDENT WOMAN

Spinning on the periphery, you dance
domestic steps to your own odd music.
Now at odds with old friends, now
out of sorts with yourself, you talk
gingerly, out of respect
for whatever you may do next.

Watching their eyes, you try to guess
what they expect of you,
what they suspect.
Suspended in your own animation,
you depend upon their
steady conversation.

What will you do next?
What will you say?
You toe-dance lightly on the edge
of their marriage,
their apparently happy children,
wishing them the best,

but not wanting it for yourself.
You know it would be better
if you could excuse yourself,
refusing a third brandy
saying, "It's too late.
I've got to take the baby-sitter home."

FAT ANN COMES HOME

Fat Ann hearkens to the jackals.
When the desert dogs laugh
she recalls being slim.
That rarely. Rousseau caught
her one evening (you've not
seen that picture) on the Kalahari
under a full moon, slender
young as a dream and dark.
Fat Ann hearkens to the snicker
of a finger flicking off the light.
She remembers, then,
a hurried hand trembling
her flat stomach like a flamenco
dancer tapping love
on a cold, black floor in Salamanca.
Fat Ann hearkens to her own back
door slammed by the idiot's
guffaw, the spinster's chuckle,
"Here's my precious cat," called
hopeless after midnight in Nebraska.

THE HANFORD WIVES

East of us the vineyards grow
in orderly rows,
trellised for full exposure
to our quick summers.
Here in Richland, Kennewick, Pasco,
suburbs of a city that does not exist,
we study our lives
in brief verses,
we, the Hanford wives.

In summer the amaranth and artemisia
slip into our yards
leaving their common names
(tumbleweed, sagebrush) like the names
of old lovers
irrevocably seeded.
We pretend not to notice,
tell our husbands to mow the lawn
quick, before something gets hold.

Dust can storm in here
from any direction, blotting the sun.
North of us something
more unstable than ourselves
happens in a language
even the sun would not understand.
Bees keep my husband occupied
when he's not with the reactor.
The children love it.

MOON WOMAN

I have seen them scream in silence
when your lips clinched,
when your fingers
clutched an empty cigarette pack
twisting the cellophane
like a swan's neck.
Then, you were dark Hekate.

Or I have seen them close their eyes
in ecstasy when you smiled,
when your finger
drew the sweat straight down the side
of a cool brown bottle
and kissed it to your lips for jealousy.
Then, you were sweet Selene.

Or I have seen them dance for chastity
when you would speak with men,
when your fingers
gripped some alien wrist
with unfamiliar passion in your fist
like the viscera of a dead stag.
Then, you were invincible Diana.

And I have seen them drawn with pain
when your chair was vacant,
when your fingers
failed to hold your secret
and you succumbed
like a dumb fish to your own phase.
Then, you were crazed Luna.

VISIT TO THE FIRE STATION

Today her class visited the fire station,
learned about playing with matches
and how to dangle from a second-floor
window and drop
like a rag doll
into her mother's peonies,
which will light the way with their
white blooms.

But night is dangerous, she says.
That is when the frayed lamp cord
flares up, when the heater explodes,
when the spark from the chimney
smoulders,
and daddy's old paint rags
roar into flame.
We place a wet washcloth by her bed,
leave the window open.

Below her window the peonies blossom
in soft white pillows.

HIDE-N-SEEK

Kimberley always counts too fast, afraid
when she turns around and opens her
half-shut eyes she will not even see
a small foot twitch the lower branch
of the lilac bush, or sense the nervous
grip of Jennifer's fingers on the old
half-rotted pie apple tree, or even
hear the subtle gasps of breath withdrawn
from the air. And everything will darken.

When she hides she steers clear of that place
under the wheelbarrow in a black corner
of the garage where small gray spiders
annihilate flies and hold dried bees
fading in dusty webs, or that place
near the dense forsythia where she might
slither in a coil so tight and so obscure
her sister might not find her,
or might send her *one-two-three,* shrill and sudden,
shivering across her bare shoulders.

When she seeks she looks for open space
as if her friends would wrap themselves
in sun or sprawl like spokes
among the dandelions. If they are hidden well
it might be better not to find them,
let them smile or tremble in whatever shade
they have secured. Kimberley doesn't like
surprises, doesn't like the silence of still
breathless forms, her sister hanging from a tree

like moss, friends like lizards lurking
in stone shadows, all their dread
drawn up around them like scaly skin.

For her the joy of this game only comes
with shrieks of *home-free,* swift
transitions into tag, shift
of quiet smiles to laughter, lift
of voices into lively leap-frog,
hop-scotch, jump-rope twirling light.

NOT TO WORRY

By the way, that seven year-old girl
was found this evening
unmolested in her strawberry
red sweater,
               her skyblue eyes
still unexperienced.
               That empty lot
where the chest-high thistle
should have been cut,
where those old ovens
should have been hauled off ages ago
               was not where she was.
Remember that effete stamp collector
whose fingers twitched?
The one whose empty eyes
pressed against thick
black-rimmed glasses? The one
who bought Suzy the popsicle
that day?
               He was visiting his mother
in Nebraska.
               Contrary to earlier reports,
the girl's parents were not divorced,
but are planning to vacation
at the Grand Canyon.
               She was next door
all the time, eating cookies
with a wonderful old Lutheran lady
who collects salt and pepper shakers,

plays the piano and keeps
tropical fish.
                        The old lady has no warts
on her fingers,
but she speaks with a slight Latvian accent.
She says her name is Madame Rasputin
and she is waiting for a visit
from Madame Blavatsky and the Czar.

ASOTIN GIRL STILL LOST

When the Ferris wheel pins itself to the moon
a twelve year-old girl might pass
for a woman.
                 Pedaling her bike along
Snake River, Christine might see the moon
trickling downstream, feel
                       that sudden response
to the moon
and rear up high on the pedals and sing
rare tunes like a Danish merry-go-round.

Then she would peel herself away from
farmboys' animals lowing at the moon
in their ribbon-blue
simplicity, as if a lucky cast of glossy eyes
or human-sounding notes
                   might save their throats.
Christine, you rode The Hammer
                     throwing your glad
screams into a night of men and moons.
You were young and old at once.

What happened later, when the gears of The Whip
stiffened?
            I think, Christine, you heard the moon
ring out eternity,
and your bicycle sliced its choppy trail,
               its river-silky light,
               its doubtful path,
like a hand over a mouth.

PSYCHIC JOINS SEARCH FOR MISSING GIRL

I see black water and a rippled moon
lying flat, and maybe, yes, a boulder
in the middle, a heavy log
washing hard against its shoulder.

Tell the sheriff to leave the room.

I hear laughter, a man, a woman,
farm boys bellowing, girls in satin jackets
squealing, the prize bull, the Angus calf,
the loser stirring the dirt, the girl
screaming, the roar of the Zipper
hurtling bright lights up and down
the night, the girl screaming.

No. He must stay out.

I see my father's face
among the pastries.
Black wreaths float
among the loaves.

I feel the patient water,
gentle flesh, the caress of fishes,
bones settling down,
I'm sorry, ooze
and quiet silt,
and the drifting away forever.

AFTER THE RAIN

Savage birds scatter bright apples
into the deep cheatgrass.
A young woman scares the meadowlarks,
magnifies her solitude
with her own voice.
Overhead brave sparrowhawks quarrel
with raucous crows
twice their size.
Behind her an owl
groans for the setting sun.
Bright apples, bright apples
glow in her lonely arms.

RIVER SCENE

Silent mullein shivers near an old woman's
gray shack on the Salmon.
In the loam of her garden
supple daffodils tease
dry cornstalks,
absurd as a girl's laughter
echoing in the canyon's marrow,
craving a lover.

TOWN LIBRARIAN

Ethel Magruder's teeth click
through chicken salad sandwiches thick
with mayonnaise. "Be still,"
she whispers from behind her winesap.
Her eyes glaze, if only they could kill.
Her own waxed paper rattles in her lap.

To the right of her brown bag,
adult fiction hovers like a hag
over a cauldron. Across the hall
adult non-fiction rests
unmolested, Gibbon's *Decline and Fall,*
Grant's *Memoirs*, Dewey's *Quest.*

When her eyes blink
on the apple, children slink
into Commager's *Blue and Gray*
with the Brady pictures,
scattering to their proper place
when the waxed paper stirs.

Checking out *The Sea for Sam*, you wonder
about those violent forbidden men at Sumter,
those yawning eyes at Malvern Hill,
that icy drummer boy buried at Shiloh,
Ethel Magruder, alone with Henry Miller,
alone with the icy drummer boy.

ESTELLE'S ANTIQUES

In a good antique shop where the owner's so old
she doesn't care what it's all worth,
blurred Meakin trademarks, that walnut cradle
dovetailed by the Shiloh veteran,
dowled tables lurking cherry
beneath the cracked shellac, you can
bargain if you can remember the weather.

Deep in the brass tick of that Seth Thomas clock,
delicate in the blue Limoges cameo
her memory stirs for something hers,
but nothing rises. Vague violins of rain.
The snow, the tautological leaves.

You did not know her husband, and her sons
are grown and gone. Only she
remains, dried asters,
faded carnations, brittle zinnias
beneath the horrid endurance of dusty bell jars.

AN AMERICAN GRANDMA FORESEES HER DEATH

Grandma, in *True Confessions,* in love's
blissful lingerie, manicured fingers
loosening silk brassieres,
good boys going off to unambiguous war,
flak over the Ruhr,
depressed surgeons leaving neurotic wives
for love, for someone like you, Grandma,
obscurity and bliss in Florida,
Grandma, it was never like this.

When was it you stopped believing what you read,
found no other gods, stopped knitting afghans,
found an old man in your bed
disguised as your husband?
When was it death
began to whisper at your crocheted edges?

Suddenly you cannot turn the pages.
Grinning physicians mock your dreams.
Your teeth rattle
like someone else's teeth,
and if you turn the page, what then?
You reserved your life for love,
learning to hate nothing.
Now what do you have to greet this confusion?
Central Florida's finest collection
of salt and pepper shakers.

AT THE NURSING HOME

Here is an old wife awaiting death.
She has refined her life
to one story
              with gestures.
How she canned vegetables one fall
enough to last the snow all winter
              in central Idaho
when her sister was there.
She tells it again
as her fingers stir the air
            peeling apples,
            snapping beans,
            slicing carrots.
Again that legend. John, her husband,
            loved his applesauce.
Only one jar failed to seal.

LONG-TIME RESIDENT PASSES AWAY

Gladys, Ethel, Irma,
Opal, Ruby, Pearl,
we meet your glittering yesterday names
today in the obituary section.
You were Walter's wife, or Herman's,
or nobody's. All your life
you taught school,
waited tables,
sold negligees.
Yourself, you wore flannel, gingham,
vague pastels.
Now we see you in an early photograph,
lusterless already at thirty,
your life
settled about you
like dust on plastic flowers.
What did peonies glazed with April showers
mean to you, or frost
murdering young roses,
you who died of natural causes?

The Husbandman, a.. *'s ow the Seeds* ;
Hnd, then, on Hope, *till* Harvest, *feeds.*

FAMILY CAMP NEAR BELMONT, OHIO 1948

When my clean cousin joined us in our foxhole
where we brought war to southeast Ohio
Uncle Craig would be along as sure as yellow jackets
in the privy.
"Your aunt," my father used to say,
"won't even let him drink a beer."
Because of Grandpa whom I never knew
because the Depression gulped him down,
his lumberyard and all his stocks and bonds.
So Uncle Craig would hoist my cousin
from our dusty pit and we'd pretend
the Germans got him.

Later, after the fine clank of horseshoes,
a real man's game, the steel,
the lack of subtlety, the only game
where a near miss is good, Grandpa
must have loved it,
we would sit outside and eat our soft
yet strangely cold hand-cranked ice cream
while bold flies
danced across the apple pies.

Then Uncle Craig, his voice
rasping August, the locusts
humming with him, one of them off key,
would sweep his palm across the table
scattering flies and women.
He'd do it once or twice,
and then, "Good God, Craig," my father used to say,
"don't blame the flies."

FROST WARNING

After midnight the bright moon
teases me from bed like a rumor.
Full of innuendo and pale light,
the moon insinuates it is the lover
of my garden. Its cold rays
play among the tomatoes, seize
the last beans shriveling like green
penises on the dying vines, fondle
the riches of the crook-necked squash
I left to ripen one more day.

Strange cuckold, I stumble outside
guided by vague notions of honor,
reputation. Grass and weeds thrust
and twine among the neglected vegetables.
In the shadows I pull snaky
morning-glory from the strangled throats
of my squash. My icy fingers race
to save the tomatoes before they are
touched irrevocably. The second crop
of corn will not make. Already
the cukes grow bitter. In bed
my sweet wife dreams of an old lover
whose name she cannot remember.

OCTOBER SOIREE

I nightmare a gray orgy,
bland shirts striped a muted blue
and cheese-poked mouths
strumming The Department
like an old guitar.

On the cutting-board my hand
tightens into a roll of salami
hard and garlic strong
against the talk and talk
about the talk. Suddenly
they all get subjunctive,

could, and should, and if
I were
I would.
Then the women cross their legs
in unison, intransitive,
feet dangling.

The beer turns indefinite.
The wine runs free
as an idle memory.
I remember when every fool
I made of myself was funny.
I tell myself over and over.
"Bring on the hard stuff," I say,
somebody's face going gray
as my dream.

Someone's sinuous fingers
float to the sour cream.
Behind me the music
hums like a bloated locust,
remnant of summer
gone fat on the fondue.

Spinning, I grab the nearest breast.
"Any port in a storm!" I shout
above her shriek. Feet shuffle,
lights go out. The last voice
is the chairman crooning like an old movie,
"If you believed in me."

THERE'S SOMETHING SUSPICIOUS

All my life I've been followed.
Black Buicks with dark-haired
vaguely foreign men
flex the highway behind me.
At night their headlights
probe my spine like fingers
tightening a sponge.

In winter footprints trace the snow
around my house.
My neighbor says it's just the dogs,
some mastiff breed with nondescript paws.
My neighbor
speaks with a strange accent.
Blue-eyed, he's the right age
for an old Gestapo agent.
Lately he's taken to wearing black
calf-length leather coats.

When I'm gone they'll find
my drawers stuffed with odd
keys. These will fit
uncertain doors, deposit boxes,
lockers at bus terminals
in small towns, ignitions of red
Alfa-Romeos, sky-blue Maseratis.

When I'm gone they'll find
my drawers crammed with
unfinished poems, subtle evocations,

passionate shudders, profane breaths:
"The rat crawled up her . . . "
sordid spaces. See?
Those aliens in big cars,
those leathered men who plod
about my house on snowy nights, they'll see,
they'll see there's more to all this
than meets the eye.

TELLING THE FUTURE

In this photograph all my children
have noses,
              even the bewildered baby,
my button-nosed son.
Seeing his sisters
              I know he'll
grow out of it,
              establishing the family nose
like a business.
              My father had a nose
for business, but he never sniffed
the sweet perfume
              of success.
Left that to me, he said once,
and the grandchildren.
              He loved to sneeze
terribly from his good Scottish nose
during slow days
              when pollen
hung in the humid air
like grudging customers
              slow
with their dollars.
              My daughters
will marry good, small-nosed men
whose fortunes are nothing to sneeze at.
Everyone says my son
looks like his mother.

COMPOSTING AT FORTY

You thought, just after dawn
to belly up in your great green
gorging truck, as you've always done,
and cram the rinds of my oranges,
succulent honeydew, exotic coffee grounds
into your iron maw.
No more. Now I'm plowing it all back in,
reinvesting it along with rotten apples,
maple leaves, grass clippings, cigarettes
and other bad old habits
in this bank of dirt.
I am cultivating a new reverence
for the undevoured, for all the small
unsavory things of the earth,
for all the half-cooked peas,
burnt beans, stale crusts of bread, eggshells.
By God
they shall be nobly put to use
through intercession of the acids,
friction, heat, the weight of soil,
rain and melting snow dissolving
their weak identities
for a new, rich, dark and fertile earth.

WAITING FOR SNOW
DECEMBER 7, 1981

Tonight wind rips through the ranks of wheat
waiting for live burial,
sure of resurrection and reaping.
Unsleeping, I pretend to wake up in Hawaii,
surf hissing warm, the air
smelling of sunny pineapples.
My neighbor's radio
plays "Sun Valley Serenade" and I think
how odd it would be to live in Idaho again
this time of year,
wheat shoots inching over muddy hills
waiting for snow.

Maybe I'm going to college,
visiting a friend from the Islands, a Jap.
His parents are polite but their English
is worse than Charlie Chan's.
As the first wave of aircraft
drones over the *Arizona,*
I am falling in love with his sister.
She says they are Japanese.

Her English is wonderful
sounding like gentle rain
in an oriental garden, the two of us
embracing under the red lacquered bridge.

As the first bombs drop
she tells me about the bonsai.
I tell her about spring wheat

growing in the snow.
The rest of this is black and white
like old photographs, newsreels, memories.
Tomorrow I enlist.

HAWTHORNVILLE

I want to live in a dying town
among gray buildings drying in the sun,
along oak shrouded boulevards
where bricks disintegrate
from gnarled roots, decaying leaves
and unevaporated rain,
and mold is the primary smell
and black is the primary tint.
The taste would be old blood
and the touch would be the cool
of faded silk in the shade
or the crustiness of rusty tools.
I want to live in a dying town
unfunctional as a twice-bent nail,
where broken houses
through their windows frown
and Mason jars go purple in the light,
but not an empty place
of desolate foundations.
Live worms must writhe after the rain
and spiders spin at night,
thistles and briarberries mingle everywhere
with morning-glory vines
blossoming at dawn
amid upthrusting mushrooms
in this dying town
in which I want to live.

LOST AND FOUND

Tonight my yard hardens
under an icy moon.
Lying softly in bed
I cannot dream away
my confusion.
Endless forests of overgrown
Christmas trees sway
rhythmically.
"This way," they whisper,
"this way to the road,
this way out of the woods."
I measure a large tree,
topple it,
trim the stump,
hoist it over my slim shoulders.
Drunk on the cold air
I weave knee-high in crusty snow
back to where the car should be
if it had any sense,
but it doesn't.
Bear left at an angle.
With any luck
the crest of the next hill
should show me
all the answers.

Now is a good time
to set down the tree and shout
if only for the echo's sake,
losing dignity
like a leather glove that was old

anyway.
Let the tree
root itself in the snow,
let it flourish again come spring.
Just a saw and a hatchet,
no matches to slow me down.
Clip a few branches,
place them lengthwise
under a generous cedar
and wait out the night.
Better to stay in one place
at a time.
Let the sheriff show what he can do,
let the loggers
load me onto their snowmobiles
and carry me into town
for laughs at the local bar,
or let me stagger onto the highway
days later, survivor
thanks to my Boy Scout training.

Keep moving in cold weather,
especially when you are soaked
with anxious sweat,
or settle down
to keep whatever heat
your body decides you're worth.
Find a stream
running downhill faster than you dare;
follow it as deer and elk have
leaving their tracks
like the signatures of wise men.
Now in a broad meadow of snow

the stream flows into a creek.
Where old stumps
break a field
at chainsaw height
I discover a logging road
offering four directions.
Guess, walk a hundred yards,
and guess again.
Decide. Listen for the growl
of a hunter's pick-up,
with any luck
swaying low along the ruts,
coming to carry me home.

Strangely disappointed now
I squirm in the warm blankets.
In the basement my wet shirt
churns in the washer,
my boots dry fast by the heater
like frightened mouths,
hollow,
unable to scream.
This night I might have
communed with the cold,
watched my flannel shirt
stiffen with frost,
felt my lungs draw ice,
my breath grind to a halt,
sleep coming easily.

Of Little-Gaines, *let Care be had* ;
For, of small Eares, *great* Mowes *are made.*

REMAINS OF ICARUS UNCOVERED

Last week we found the bones of Icarus
a few miles west of Pine Bluff, Arkansas.
He'd blown that far off course
(so much for navigating by the stars,
or by one star, at least, the high-strung sun).
We thought at first to keep the whole thing
secret, not to tell a soul,
but someone pointed out we had a grant,
let myth or history come to what it will,
that we were obligated to fulfill
our contract, no matter
what the indirect expense.

Perhaps the island of Icaria
will have to be renamed,
or maybe Arkansas.
Ovid's *Metamorphoses,* book eight, must be
revised to show a sudden gust of wind,
and then a long slow glide
across the Continental Divide.

We figure Daedalus buried his son
deep in this bank of clay.
That's what preserved his bones and the print
of his outstretched pinions,
somewhat seared and missing some key feathers.
Carbon dating shows the thousands of years
involved, and what could be petrified tears.
What cinched it was the set of his mouth
and the sockets of his eyes
doubly enlarged in terrified surprise.
"The story we were told was art,"
I tell my students, "science never lies."

69

FONK'S GOES UNDER

When the last dime store went under
prices dived for days. Shoppers
strange to the manager seeped
in, then poured until
he propped the doors open,
fore and aft, and still they streamed
in from the parking lot,
in from the street,
in from shopping centers outside town.

At first the counters held,
Duvella's luncheonette to port,
men's sportshirts starboard,
hardware, toys and tropical fish
for ballast.
But then the galley cooled.
Duvella told the reporter
about those young couples and the war,
the mirror with Guadalcanal dead
reflected when she turned
from certain faces to her grill.

Without Duvella the store listed badly,
took on too much empty
space. Slowly the salesgirls
abandoned their posts
slipping away after five not to return,
replaced by the stern manager,
face hardening to his martyrdom.

At last prices floundered and the store
filled with the smell of dust

and cold popcorn.
Plastic firetrucks with missing wheels,
tin boats without motors,
unmatched socks and empty hangers,
these were the flotsam on a slick
of memories and outdated profits.

At Main Street's edge
oldtimers gather reminiscing of oiled floors,
propeller fans, Duvella,
the old man whose son tried hard
but didn't have it, the new manager,
what was his name?
went down with the last dime store.

A DREAM OF SHERBET

The poet dreams of sherbet.
Reluctant to discuss this
cold subject with even his closest protégée,
he carries it with him
like a deep colorful symbol.

His writing improves.
Love glows lemon bright in his odes.
Pure pineapple sorrow
grieves in his lines.
Critics applaud his
raspberry overstatement,
his subtle orange, his vivid lime.
He dares to be guava.
Daiquiri dances from stanza to stanza.

One night he dreams
a torrid mamey in Havana,
his cone heaped too high.
He grabs at the melting sherbet
cramming it back,
but all around him
slim-waisted women laugh,
wide-eyed children
blow cigar smoke into his
sticky face.

Now he cannot awaken.
Sherbet squeezes between his fingers,
oozes onto the sheets
staining their whiteness

with wonderful colors.
Now he feels bad about Castro.
He regrets Honduras, El Salvador, Mexico,
the United Fruit Company,
the Organization of American States,
the Pan-American Conference of 1923,
the Monroe Doctrine.

Now the ghost of Che Guevara
climbs into the poet's bed.
"Hombre," he says, "do not forget me.
When they shot me in Bolivia
I was eating papaya sherbet
with a small wooden spoon.
I was so innocent!"

But then Alfredo Stroessner
kicks Che out of bed.
"Listen to me gringo," he snarls,
"I have read Neruda, Marquez, Borges.
Also I have eaten rainbow sherbet
on a hot humid day
floating down the Paraná,
river of corpses.
Do not think these nightmares
will redeem you.
All of them dreamed of sherbet.
These days no one is innocent.

THE CRUISE MISSILE

In terms you will understand,
this missile will proliferate
like dandelion fluff on a spring
breeze. Death and life,
pardon the ironies.
In terms of accuracy,
consider children on a street
corner of a small town,
a small street, small
children playing jacks;
consider, not those static jacks,
but the bouncing red
rubber ball, those small fists
flicking in the sun.
Pardon the sentiment.
In terms of cost, this missile
sells itself.
Let's say a studio in Balboa,
off the beach, New Orleans
in late January, one week alone
in Nantucket. Pardon the confusion.
In terms you will understand,
this missile will rise from its pad
like a virile lover
stepping into his trousers with a smile.

RAINSTORM

Yesterday afternoon a sudden rainstorm
twisted maple limbs across random lines
slipping some of us into darkness for hours,
others for only minutes or quick
blinking seconds. We have aromatic candles,
a large glass kerosene lamp,
smokeless oil that smells vanilla,
fatal if swallowed.
Some were not so lucky.

Between torrents I watched the old minister
who wears white patent shoes
move his rocking chair,
gift of his congregation,
into the Mayflower van, and he
only a Methodist.
"Promoted," he said sadly,
and suddenly it rained to beat hell.

Streets don't drain well here.
Coming back from the store
I saw a motorcyclist sputter
halfway through a knee-deep intersection.
His feet heaved up to the handlebars,
so the cycle just keeled over
taking him with it
into the muddy water. To hear that
sudden end of noise and see him

splash like a stunned fish
gave me renewed faith in rain.

Today my garden makes new green covenants.
Now the tomatoes, squash and beans
are showing me something. The lettuce
threatens to bolt.
The new minister wears running shoes
and his bitter son
drives a new red Yamaha.
Tonight lively unscented lights
will burn steadily all over town
and reception will be good everywhere.

"A MULTITUDE OF BIRDS"
-St. Francis of Assissi

Sing now the desperate dance of small birds.
Sing where the quail collect after snowfall,
the mud-gutted borders of roads where the last
hard grains of wheat lay heaped with the gravel.

Sing the wren's last colorless song,
the solitary vireo's slow cold slur
by the roadside sifting old brown bags
for crusts or breadcrumbs, or perhaps

among the shards of bright green glass
a sip of wine, a claret deep as blood.
Sing then the cunning of sparrows which look
like nothing but dark little rocks,

for they will endure, and the starling
whose song is the echo of anything,
and the waxwing, gregarious feeders.
Sing warblers and blackbirds perched on the edge

of winter with ice clinging fast
to their wings, with plentiful seed
lying deep, with songs frozen hard into words,
sing now the desperate dance of small birds.

TOWARD WINTER

Dirt and gravel bleed through sycamore leaves.
Buckeyes grieve for their lost sheen.
In numb November a gray dream
sharp as a broken jar
concealed in a leaf-trap
leaps in the gaunt air against the garage
where a cold mattress
leans like an old whore.

Newpapers age suddenly, grip the curb,
stiff pages quavering, athletes,
soldiers, rebels, debutantes
frozen together.
In this precise weather
a crazed rubber ball sags impotent
against itself
like a collapsed lung.

CHILD'S BACKYARD IN WINTER

Beneath the leafless appletree the sand
congeals in its wooden frame
freezing her casual pail-shaped castle,
the destined summer residence
for the czar of all Russias.

Her swing hangs rigid,
link soldered to link, a crystal statue
formed of steel and solid water
that soared to supple mach twelve
thirty days ago.

Her jumprope slung over the clothesline
is like summer hung out to dry,
caught in winter,
now braided ice
with cold red handles clacking in the wind.

REMEMBERING THE CITY

Foolish, the way this April snow
defies the yellow crocuses,
spatters heaped cornstalks awaiting fire
with its cold and spiteful winter spit.
This time of year winter becomes ridiculous,
like an old woman in a red fedora
cursing the curb, swearing this time
she will not vote.

So the city returns in this white April blur
ludicrous in its pain,
so out of place in this garden of mud,
dry stalks, dissolving snowflakes,
memories of a boy heaped beneath a urinal,
head deep in his hands as if he had no face.

Sudden confusion of sun.
The snow continues, unaware.
The crocuses, a yellow stare at the garden's edge,
bend to the light. What tribe is this
in the square? Blackfoot, Quinault, the Pawnee
warrior calls himself a Sioux.
Why don't they smile like other drunks do?
Suddenly unaware of seasons, returning birds
take them by surprise.
They used to know this time of year.

Now a paunchy gray cloud crosses the sun,
spurts soft pellets of hail
against the flowers, but they've seen it before,

the last flourishes of winter.
At the sidewalk cafe a one-legged pigeon
begs for crumbs, corpulent in the city
where these robins wouldn't last a day.

Whil'ſt I, the Sunne's *bright* Face may *view*,
I *will no meaner* Light *purſue.*

PALOUSE HISTORY

The history of wheatfields
is not easily written.
Mostly it's wind
and the movements of dust,
shifting of snow.
From below the surface
rocks and stones
keep edging up
as if they had
something to mutter to the sun.
Local history
comes and goes
in the stubble.
Like old men and women
each crop thinks
it has something new to tell.
Here and there a shotgun shell,
a tuft of feathers
offer their temporary testimony.
One of the stones
may be an arrowhead.
On the rocky cilia
broken trucks and plows,
weathered combines
rust peacefully.
Board by board, roofs first,
old barns and houses collapse.
The wheatfields
write a quiet book,
only the cries of hawks and mice
for punctuation.

VARIATIONS ON A LOGGER STALKED BY A COUGAR

Cougar steps from a stand of tamarack
and in his eyes red flannel
dances to a foreign tune.
No subtlety in this human song,
no long winters spent in drifts
or deep in caves or cliffs,
yet some enchantment of this tired
whistling draws him on
and closer to the unfamiliar smell.

At any moment man could turn,
behind him find the cougar
step for step and face
confronting unfamiliar face.
Then would his music end,
or would he know to bend his tune
around the tendons
stretched and nervous,
taut as a well-rehearsed sonata?

In an instant man could raise a gun
or step once backwards, run, his whistle
dying in the corridor of cougar's ear.
Or in an instant fear
might wrap his ankles,
share his lips, devour note by note
his tired throat,
leaving only scraps of shirt,
some bones, the resonance, the intervals.

NO DEMAND

Twenty years ago there was maybe sixty gypos
between Clarkia and Helmer, Bovill,
over around Potlatch. Maybe a hundred.
Ten-twenty trucks apiece, couple loaders,
get yourself a crew,
couple fellers'll cut first
drink later,
you could do business.
Hell, nobody ever got rich at it,
only the mills, but it beats a desk.
By God dangerous, too.
Keep your wits about you,
keep your head screwed on.
You'd be surprised how easy,
just a glance at a ground squirrel
at the wrong time,
widow-makers, broke chains,
some damn green kid riding a Cat
don't know shit from Shinola
buries your best friend
before you can blink the sweat from your eyes.
And suddenly you remember
you heard his last word,
"Hey!"
Colder'n a witch's teat, or hot,
raw dust sucking your lungs,
and the women get tired of it
tired of you, tired of your snoose.
My old lady up and flushed
a whole can of Copenhagen

down the toilet, brand new.
That done it.
So you don't get nowhere,
and if you've got kids
they don't amount to nothing,
teacher says they oughta go to college.
Then's when you get laid off,
wonder where the money went.
Boss says he's sorry, says
you always busted your gut,
says you'll be the first called back,
says it to the next five guys as well.
Now there couldn't be no more than twenty
and some of them down pretty low,
gypos, what the hell. No demand.
Got arthritis in both hands
so bad I couldn't set a choker,
back's no good,
I'd go back in a minute if I could.

CAL BURLESON CROWNS IDAHO COUNTY JUNIOR MISS

"Seems like towns was always burnin up back then.
Florence went up with the old Commercial Hotel.
Salesman or something, I reckon,
smokin in bed. Never smoke in bed
without a good woman to tell you when to put it out."

He cackles. The girl edges away.
She wishes they would snap the picture
and haul this old logger
back to whatever tree they found him in.
She tries for a crosscut grin.

The old man reaches around her waist
like a choker cinching up a Douglas fir.
She flinches, slips her elbow down
against his ribs, and wonders how old men like this,
the age of their whiskey's proof, can stay so frisky.

"Ain't nothin left of Florence like she was
except that cemetery off of Water Street.
After the fire they buried the sweetest whore
west of the Divide right alongside
of old Schumacher's wife.
Missouri Lutheran. He was the minister."

In the picture she leans away from old Cal
like a sapling sprouted from a half-burnt stump.

BAD LUNCH AT COTTONWOOD, IDAHO

Where wheat laps gently at the city limits
avoid seafood, even tuna salad,
and smiling waitresses
graduated from high school directly
into nylon dresses with large pockets
jangling at the waist.
                    In Seattle
there was only the soft rustle of currency
on satin, and the sound of seawater rushing
through barnacles, and the waitress was old,
efficient and hopeless.
                    Ironmonger to all
Southeast Ohio, my father taught me
to trust Businessman's Specials
when the chips are down, in restaurants
where orange plastic splits in booths
and the varnish glues your napkin
to somebody's phone number. Beware
of sticky saltshakers. Beware
of waitresses with crooked teeth. Beware
of hamburger with a nom-de-plume.
                    Cottonwood is no place
for Salisbury Steak of dubious gravy
or Salmon Croquettes torn from the sea's dark womb.

THIRTY MILES TO THREE FORKS

The only way into these ruts is a wrong
turn. On out this road three riverbeds
meet in dry humor,
goats lap alkali
                    from unslippery rocks,
the ghosts of trout meander
in your sagebrush-bitter memory.
     You've seen this sort of mockery
before, the sort that starts somewhere,
then angles off.
                    The bunkhouse, reduced
to a cord of weathered wood, leans drunkenly
against a poplar.
                    The riverbed
gutters three ways, as promised. The goats
scatter in natural fear of lost strangers.
     To laugh it off you turn back to the highway
where jack rabbits die so flat
hawks don't even dip in recognition.

THE ARCHAEOLOGIST IN THE WHEATFIELD

"Primitive man was here," he says
sweeping the flint across his sleeve,
casual as a surgeon rinsing fear.
"Here's where he struck off chips
to make spearheads, scrapers, implements."
His voice tapers off
by several thousand years,
his shotgun drops unfired across his arm,
his fingers forget the trigger for the stone.
"Of course there was no wheat then,"
he remarks vaguely,
tossing the rock across the furrow.
"They were all hunters,
too free to watch a seed grow."

BATTLE SCENE

In art each part is subordinated
to the whole. The color red
of Custer's blood must be
modulated to the flow of his hair,
and that to the undulance of hills,
and that to the stillness a dead horse
makes in the blue Montana air.
It is hard to draw ambitions true to life
when they look so much like death,
or smoke rising from a Springfield.
Dreams drop easily from the back
of a staggered Appaloosa. Feathers
drift in the dust.

TRAIL OF TEARS

These are Nez Perce, the flat
dark ones, almost circular.
Spokane speckles her sidewalks
with them, east of the Ridpath
where red and yellow signs
glare like warpaint.

When you turn from the tainted
lips of the roundfaced woman
whose pocketbook holds no medicine,
you see them like trodden wads
of gray gum, wherever you go.
That pinkish trace
is Chippewa, drawn like a moccasin
out of place, cold and spiritless
on this manufactured stone.
And these are not alone.

Beyond their range two Cheyenne
braves leave dark tears,
small and hard, along this trail.
Some Colville boys laugh soft
tears along the path
in search of the Kiowa girl
who broke their hearts with her
slim waist and white dreams.

You trace them all,
those tears of accusation
leading everywhere, on Grand
across the bridge this time,

collecting thick and cloying
under the rail as your heart
strikes and your fingers
scale them away. They slip
into the river.
Corpulent mallards eat each one,
their bright orange webs
at home here.

At night, when the sidewalks darken,
tears are memories,
like the feel of a tomahawk
to the brown hand
gripping the neck of a green bottle.

AT THE GOLDEN WEST MOTEL

We haul ourselves a long way
compressed in my old Chevrolet.
Too far from our destination night and rain
draw down on us like a pair of forty-fours.

Eight of us split into two rooms
on the city's withering edge,
sagebrush and carlots, where the best motels
bloomed twenty years ago.

Across the wet highway
an old bank robbed of its dignity
plays cafe beside a radiator shop.
Afraid to be that hungry
we jail ourselves in our dark rooms.

One sixty watt bulb
gives just enough light to confuse us.
Mirthless, the bold, bronze television
squints like a cowboy's eye against the sun.
An arrow snaps, the treaty is broken.

Worried that bad pillows
make bad dreams,
we remember what the nightclerk said,
standing beneath her husband's
collection of barbed wire,
hands hard against her lean hips:
"It ain't the Ritz,
but it's clean."

OUTSIDE THE FARMERS MERCHANTS BANK OF MONTANA

Young men in raw red sideburns,
Cat hats pushed back on their solid heads,
swagger glad in their dust.
Tractors, horses, wheat, the taut
bodies of young women squirm
in their dreams. They walk hard muscled,
tall in the streets of their small town.

> They dare not grin.
> All their lives they
> will squint till stiff
> frowns fix each edge
> of lip and eye.

Behind them their fathers, gray hair
bristling in the open wind, blue eyes
turning gelid, saunter past
grumbling of busted camshafts,
price of fertilizer, something-thianon
blowing away to protect a neighbor's sagebrush
against root-rot, rust or smut.

> Their sons do not
> understand them.
> Why don't they go
> back to college?
> Each edge squint-stiff.

GOODBYE WASHTUCNA

Tumbleweed blusters across the road
as if intent on some gray mission
among green shoots of wheat.
Ditches fill with them instead of
water. The schoolbus crushes them,
leaves their spindly bones along the way,
but most of them carry on.

The farmers send their children
to Washtucna to learn things, play
football, or just grow up
in some clandestine way and go,
not causing trouble. After school
they stop for softdrinks and a game of pool,
and everything's great
except the eightball's gone,
but most of them carry on.

THE SAGEBRUSH REBELLION
for Wally Lewis

After centuries of squatting in the dry air
west of the Mississippi, tangling the wheels
of Conestoga wagons, nesting grouse,
feeding jack rabbits and desperate sheep,
the sagebrush rebelled.

It began in deep January throughout Wyoming
where the sagebrush brooded in gentle, ghostly humps
under crusted snowdrifts soiled with dirt
dredged up from its secrecy for soft coal.
The sagebrush muttered.

That spring the sagebrush increased and toughened
their silver-thorned leaves. Their delicate yellow flowers
diminished in size, faded, and dropped early,
unnoticed except by the Nevada legislature.
The sagebrush whispered,

letting the wind scatter their seeds of dissent
into the fur of jack rabbits and coyotes
to be dispersed through Utah, Colorado,
stirring their old allies, the tumbleweed.
The sagebrush hissed

like the sidewinders hidden at their roots.
By July they menaced Nampa, Boise,
burgeoning first at Garden City, that mockery

of plastic restaurants, garish cars and trailer parks.
The sagebrush rejoiced.

Onward to Oregon they spread like a horde
hungry for a homeland, bitterly resisting
fire and pesticide, grader and plow,
ignoring the monotonous cement of interstates.
The sagebrush swept

a path through Civilization, choking the ruts
of trail bikes, four-wheel-drives and recreation rigs,
intimidating entrepeneurs and speculators who wrote
anguished protests to their California congressmen.
The sagebrush laughed

and proceeded in all directions until
the Secretary of the Interior ordered
an investigation. Why had these crazy weeds
missed all the Indian reservations?
The sagebrush smiled ·

quietly and hurried on to the Cascades.
There the rebellion ceased, to let the madrone
take over. And then the prickly West,
from Bismarck to Las Vegas, rested as
the sagebrush blossomed.

IDAHO REQUIEM
For Robert Lowell

Out here, we don't talk about culture,
we think we are. We nurtured Ezra Pound
who ran from us like hell
and never came back. You
never came at all. You
will never know how clever
we never are out here.
You never drank red beer.
You never popped a grouse
under a blue spruce just because it was there.

Tell us about Schopenhauer and your friends
and fine old family. We left ours
at the Mississippi, have no names left
to drop. We spend our time
avoiding Californians and waiting
for the sage to bloom, and when it does
we miss the damn things half the time.
When a stranger comes in we smile
and say "Tell us about yourself."
Then we listen real close.

But you would say, "I've said what I have to say."
Too subtle, perhaps, for a can of beer,
too Augustan for the Snake River breaks.
But how do you know this wasn't just
the place to die? Why not have those
kinfolk ship the bones out here, just
for irony's sake? We keep things plain
and clear because of the mountains.
Our mythlogy comes down to a logger
stirring his coffee with his thumb.

101